History Of T

World Trade Center

1973-2001

BONECHI & CITY MERCHANDISE

© Copyright by Casa Editrice Bonechi - Florence - Italy
Tel.+39 055576841 - Fax +39 0555000766 - E-mail: bonechi@bonechi.it - Internet: www.bonechi.it

Publication created and designed by Casa Editrice Bonechi
Production manager: Monica Bonechi
Picture research by the Editorial Staff of the Casa Editrice Bonechi
Graphic design and make-up: Manuela Ranfagni *and* Laura Settesoldi
Cover: Manuela Ranfagni. *Editing:* Giovannella Masini

Texts by the Editorial Staff of the Casa Editrice Bonechi
Translation: Paula Boomsliter

Printed in Italy by Centro Stampa Editoriale Bonechi

ACKNOWLEDGMENTS
This book was assembled in record time, making use of the footage we all saw on television.
We have "frozen" the images in stills for all those who will visit New York in the future and will find it a changed city.
Our heartfelt thanks to all the television cameramen, photographers, and Internet sites (CNN, BBC, Time Magazine, The New York Times, Virgilio, Altavista) whence come the images on pages 16 through 31.It is our intention in the future to create, as a volume in one of our collection of books, a more complete and detailed document on the disaster that struck New York, the United States, and indeed the entire world.
The photographs on pages 20, 22 bottom left, and 28 top were taken by Maria Elena Velardi of our New York office, which is located near the site of the World Trade Center.

PHOTOGRAPHY ACKNOWLEDGMENTS
Alan Schein/NYC: *pages 4 above and bottom left, 5, 32.*
Battman Studios: *pages 6/7, 8/9.*
Photograps from the Casa Editrice Bonechi Archives, taken by Andrea Pistolesi: *pages 3, 4 bottom right, 11, 12, 13, 14, 15;* Paolo Giambone: *page 10.*
Cover: *photographs by* Andrea Pistolesi

The publisher apologizes for any unintentional omissions. We would be pleased to include any appropriate acknowledgments of which we are informed in subsequent editions of this publication.

ISBN 88-476-0997-6

* * *

Twin Towers

The impressive Twin Towers, at the southern tip of Manahattan Island between Vesey and Liberty Streets and West and Church Streets, were one of the world's largest business complexes: the World Trade Center. The idea developed in the early 1960's as part of a plan to relaunch the downtown area as an international business and financial center; in fact, the New York Stock Exchange was also originally slated to move there.

The backers reviewed hundreds of plan before they selected Minoru Yamasaki and Emery Roth as architects; actual construction work began in 1969. The Towers were built of 181,000 tons of steel; the parts were prefabricated in the Midwest US and lifted into place by eight specially-built cranes brought in from Australia. The towers of the World Trade Center opened on April 4, 1973. The I WTC tower soared to a height of 1709 feet (521 m) with its television antenna; its twin, 2 WTC to 1362 feet (415 m). Both stood on foundations sunk to a depth of 755 feet (23 m). Although the towers were not very interesting from a stylistic standpoint, they opened equipped with a state-of-the-art telecommunications

The Winter Garden

Before the disaster of September 11, 2001, the spectacular Winter Garden in the World Financial Center, adjacent to the World Trade Center, was linked to it by an elegant covered elevated passageway. The view of the Hudson River and Ellis Island from this glass and steel building was magnificent. Its high nave hosted a palm grove that served as a garden setting for the cafes, restaurants, and bookstores that surrounded it, while the unconventional semicircular staircase in red and grey marble was used as an amphitheater for many events staged in this fascinating corner of New York.

The two parallel piped towers of steel and glass that were the Twin Towers soared heavenward over the lower tip of Manhattan and for years were an essential feature of the city skyline.

system comprising the first fiberoptic audiovisual network for commercial use ever installed in the United States. The observatory on the top floor of 1 WTC offered the city's most intoxicating view of New York and the Hudson River, with Staten Island, Ellis Island, and the Statue of Liberty. The famous "Windows on the World" restaurant and cocktail lounge—one of the city's most elegant spots—was located on the 107th floor.

The World Trade Center

Before the terrorist attack of September 11, 2001, the Twin Towers 1 WTC and 2 WTC were the heart of the World Trade Center and indeed all of Lower Manhattan. They are gone.

The two towers, 110 stories and over 1,400 feet (400 m) tall, were the most striking elements in a complex of seven buildings designed by Minoru Yamasaki (1912-1986) in collaboration with a host of construction engineers. Work on the World Trade Center began in 1962 and was brought to completion 15 years later. At first the Center aroused no great enthusiasm among New Yorkers, who felt it was simply too big and that the style was too cold.

The Twin Towers alone were the workplaces of 50,000 individuals and drew 80,000 tourists a day. From the outdoor panoramic platform on the roof of 2 WTC, like from the glassed-in observation deck and restaurant on the 107th floor, about 65 feet (20 m) lower down, the views of the city and the Hudson Valley were electrifying and absolutely peerless. On a clear day you could see nearly over 50 miles (90 km) in every direction. A single ticket for the "**Top of the World**" was a visitors'

passport to three virtual adventure theaters, many InfoVision video kiosks, numerous restaurants and a souvenir shop, and the kinetic energy sculpture exhibit.

In 1993 the Twin Towers were the target of a dynamite attack against the US federal government offices located in the complex, which caused six deaths, a great many wounded, and massive physical damage.

On permanent exhibition at the World Trade Center, and precisely in the huge Austin J. Tobin Plaza in front of the Towers, were the bronze Globe by Fritz Koenig, a pyramid by Masayuki Nagare, and an Alexander Calder mobile. Since the 1993 attack on the foundations of the Towers, a monument to the memory of the victims stood in the central square.

SEPTEMBE

R 11, 2001

MANHATTAN SKYLINE

A t 8:45 a.m. on Tuesday, September 11, 2001, the unmistakable profile of downtown Manhattan changed forever.

The World Trade Center, icon of the economic power of the United States, symbol of American pride, a city rising vertically within another city, crumbled, pulverized in the span of "just" ninety minutes.

The terrifying chronicle of the most serious terrorist attack in history began in the heart of New York City, where every day fifty thousand individuals worked nine to five in offices on the 110 floors of steel and glass that were the structure of the Twin Towers; where every day eighty thousand visitors were ferried up and down the height of the towers—at the fantastic speed of about 25 feet (8m)/second—by 208 elevators.

Up there, at the top, was Windows On the World. The WTC brochure and the tourist guides proclaimed it the "world's highest restaurant," the only place to dine with your head—literally— in the clouds.
Over 1400 feet below (459 m) were all the

phantasmagoric lights of Manhattan; you could see much of the Hudson and the East River, and the Brooklyn Bridge.

From up there, even the 843 acres of Central Park looked like somebody's back yard.
Up there you couldn't help— if only for a moment—but remember King Kong and his desperate, last embrace of the towers in the remake of the movie.
Up there, inevitably, you found yourself humming a tune made famous by Liza Minnelli, because up there you really did feel you were "king of the hill, top of the heap."

Or you stopped in at the souvenir shop to take away a tiny bite of the Big Apple.
It might have been one of those plastic balls that scatter snow on a miniature Manhattan, complete with its Towers, its Empire State Building, and its Statue of Liberty all crowded together in an improbable cityscape.

Or it might have been a book, a calendar, a tee-shirt, a postcard sent to friends with a penned-in arrow pointing at the top floor to show that "we" had really been up there.

From "up there" it was great fun to look "down there" and remark on the apparent size of the cars, the people, the other buildings, which seemed so small that after a while you couldn't wait to get your feet back on the ground and resume your normal "human" proportions.
There was just one way to photograph the

Towers: to back up step by step from the World Trade Center with your camera aimed as high as it would go until they came into the viewfinder of your typical tourist camera.

The numbers that made the history and drew the portrait of the Twin Towers—their height, the number of windows, the millions of dollars spent, the tons of material, the miles of electrical cables—are worthy of entry in the Guinness Book of Records, without exception. Today they have been erased to make space for other, sinister numbers: the number of dead and wounded, the number of those who will recover, the number of people whose bodies and souls will carry the scars of that day for who knows how long.

The idea informing the work of Minoru Yamasaki, the Japanese architect who designed the towers, was that they become a concrete symbol of man's confidence in Man. In the light of the terrible events that changed Manhattan's skyline, we cannot help but ask ourselves what else collapsed at 10:07 and 10:27 on Tuesday, September 11, 2001, together with the Twin Towers of the World Trade Center.

Maybe the towers will be rebuilt. Maybe there will remain a space, an open wound, a scar to remind us of something we ought never to forget.

But even though the two skyscrapers have been as if plucked out of the Manhattan skyline, they will always remain in our hearts. No act of

barbarism, even the cruelest, can ever truly destroy the works of civilized man.

The media images of the terrorist attack in New York brought the most dramatic direct reportage of our times into everyone's homes.

At 8:45, under the astonished gazes of the thousands of people who were setting about their everyday activities on a morning seemingly just like any other, an American Airlines passenger jet hijacked by a commando unit of terrorists, veered off course and flew straight into one of the towers of the World Trade Center in the heart of downtown Manhattan.
Eighteen minutes later, while the cameras of the world's broadcasting companies were focusing on the nightmarish images of the smoke and flames

pouring out of the north tower, another plane made a direct hit on the other tower.

The two airliners had been transformed into missiles, their unaware and guiltless passengers into human warheads directed against targets filled with likewise unaware and guiltless citizens.

The death throes of the two giant buildings lasted an hour and a half. During this time, inside the towers, there were played out human dramas and tragedies later documented by the voices of the survivors, the reports of the rescue workers, the images snapped by the photographers who despite their equal sense of horror immortalized the heartbreaking

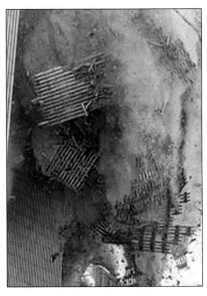

cries for help, the desperate gestures dictated by panic, the last moments in the lives of scores and scores of human beings. Many, to escape the hell of the flames, threw themselves from the windows of the upper floors.

Those ninety long minutes decided the fates of thousands of people who just because they happened to be there, on that day, at that time, trapped in what until September 11 had been an office building like any other. The lucky ones who escaped the terrible impact of the planes or who were not isolated on the top floors began the long descent to safety down the stairs: ninety minutes, an eternity for those used to a short elevator ride between their offices and the street.

At 10:07 the world watched, impotent, as the south tower collapsed, and twenty minutes later as the second of the giants fell. They were simply gone, crumbled into an immense cloud of dust and smoke that spread across New York, almost as if to piteously hide its shame.

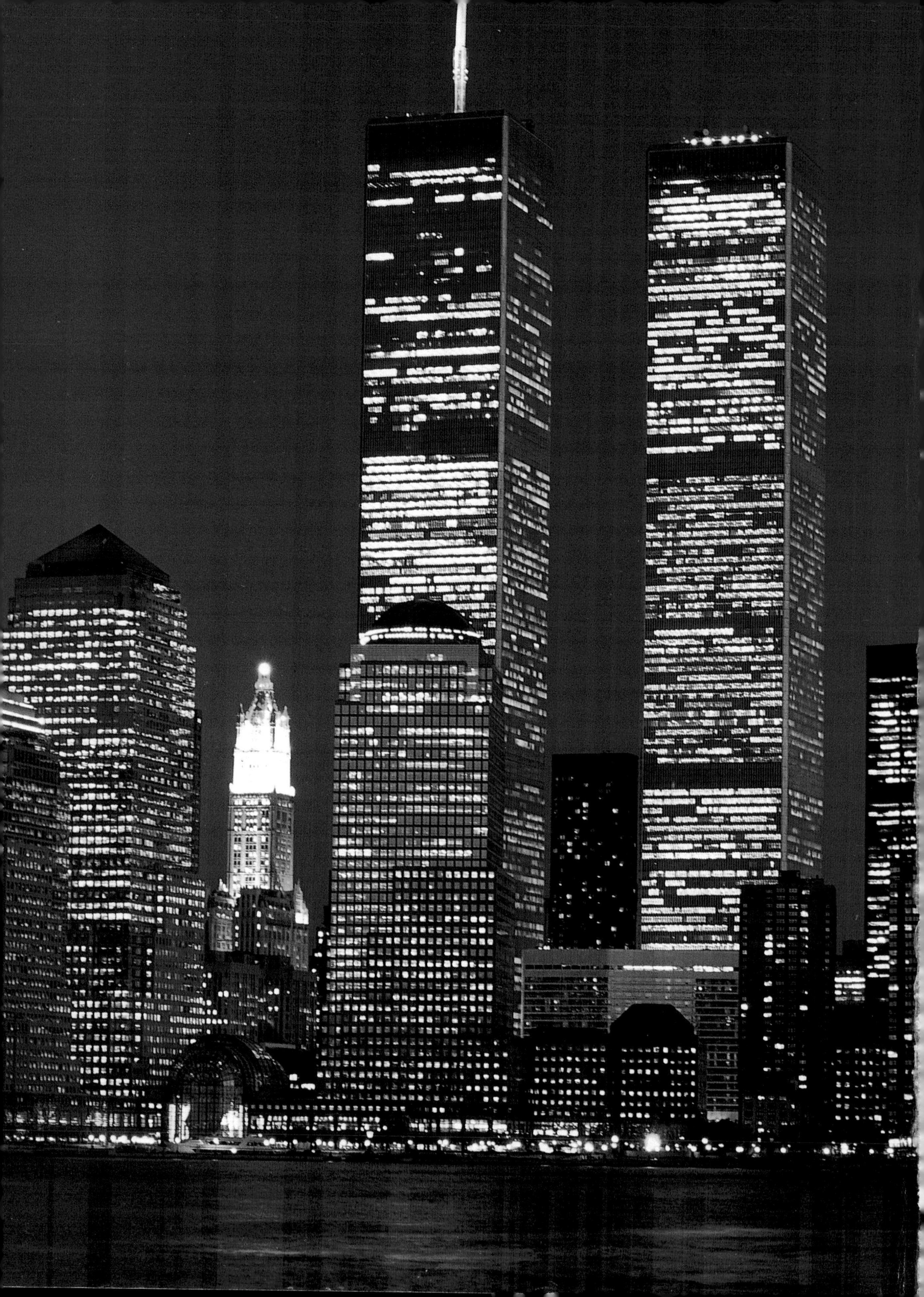